IMAGES
of England

AROUND
MORLEY

Queen St.

Cross Hall.

Howley Ruins.

Bandstand in Park.

MORLEY.

G.N Ry Station.

IMAGES
of England

AROUND
MORLEY

Compiled by
Norman Ellis

TEMPUS

First published 1998
Copyright © Norman Ellis, 1998

Tempus Publishing Limited
The Mill, Brimscombe Port,
Stroud, Gloucestershire, GL5 2QG

ISBN 0 7524 1117 9

Typesetting and origination by
Tempus Publishing Limited
Printed in Great Britain by
Midway Clark Printing, Wiltshire

Contents

Acknowledgements

The author appreciates the valuable help given by many people in the preparation of this book. Thanks especially to the staff of Morley Reference and Local History Library. Thanks to staff at Bradford and Leeds Reference and Local History Libraries and Archives.
Thanks to Bob Bennett of York and Ian Lindley of Outwood for the loan of certain material.
Much useful information was gleaned form back issues of the *Morley Observer*.

Introduction

'It is not surprising that some people regard with a jealous eye and a certain suspicion the coming of the cars.' The cars under scrutiny were tramcars, not motorcars. The words were printed in a booklet entitled, *Morley 1886-1911*, which was issued by Samuel Stead & Sons from the *Morley Observer* office, in 1911.

The critique continued, 'Morley has hitherto delighted in its independence. It has had a distinct and separate entity, with a history, traditions, characteristics of its own, and to be linked at last by tramways to a busy community and great commercial centre like the neighbouring city [Leeds] marks another and a very important change in the circumstances of the town.'

In spite of this, Morley did remain largely independent. However, in 1921, the City of Leeds submitted a scheme to absorb the Borough of Morley. After a long public enquiry, at which the Mayor of Morley, Alderman Hedley Watson, championed the Morley cause, the plan was abandoned.

No such happy outcome was forthcoming in 1974 when, via government legislation, Morley finally lost its independence and became part of the City of Leeds. What would Morley's proud Edwardians have made of this? A more recent development was the opening of the White Rose Shopping Centre, almost on Morley's doorstep. The town's former shopkeepers must be turning in their respective graves!

The history of Morley goes back to Norman, Saxon and even Roman times. However, just when the town was becoming a place of some eminence, the marauding Scots arrived, took up residence and, before leaving in 1322, destroyed the church and much of the town.

The Morley of today is largely a legacy of the Industrial Revolution. Improvements in sheep farming resulted in an abundance of wool. This led to the development of the domestic handloom cloth trade as Morley's staple industry from the sixteenth century onwards. The cloth was much in demand, some of it being sold on Leeds Bridge.

The transition from the handloom cloth trade to the steam factory system began towards the end of the eighteenth century. The two methods struggled side by side for some years.

In 1790, the town's first steam mill, known as Crank Mill, was constructed in Station Road. The mill was erected by the Earl of Dartmouth, at the request of Mr Webster, a member of an old Morley cloth-making family. Machines with strange sounding names were introduced. The 'Shake-Willy' was used to cleanse raw wool and the 'Slubbing Billy' to twist the yarn. The working classes, fearing that mechanisation would destroy their livelihoods, were sceptical of the new technology. Nevertheless, by the 1830s, Morley folk were beginning to accept the inevitable. In 1834, the large Gillroyd Mill was erected. A subsequent glut of cloth led to a slump in trade.

A turning point came with the discovery that old cloth, woollen rags and tailor's clippings could be broken down to a fibrous state and worked with new wool to produce cheaper but good quality cloths. These became known as shoddy and mungo. Morley formed part of a greater shoddyopolis, which included Dewsbury, Batley and Ossett.

Morley entered a period of almost unbroken progress. The greater acceptance of machinery, the utilisation of reclaimed wool and the introduction of cotton warps were the prelude to a boom in mill and warehouse construction. Many of the new structures, together with worker's houses, were built from locally quarried stone. Collieries in the area provided coal for industrial and domestic purposes.

A Charter of Incorporation was granted to Morley, by Queen Victoria, on 31 December 1885, which elevated the town to the status of a municipal borough. The old Local Board, consisting of twelve members, was replaced by a new Council, with a mayor, aldermen and councillors.

A coat of arms was granted to the Borough of Morley in 1887. It included two shuttles, a pick-axe and a spade, to symbolise the area's woollen, coalmining and quarrying industries.

In 1895, Morley's success was further exemplified by the opening of a fine town hall. In subsequent years, the town acquired its own electricity works, library, public baths and grammar school. Dartmouth and Scatcherd Parks were also opened.

The borough boundaries were considerably extended in 1937 to take in Drighlington, Gildersome, West Ardsley and East Ardsley. Churwell and a small segment of West Ardsley had been absorbed as early as 1891. In 1956, the Borough of Morley was divided into eleven wards, one of them being Tingley. Pictures from all the above areas are included in this book, most of them being from the pre-1937 era.

The advance of Morley's industries generated a need for better forms of transport to carry raw materials, products and workers. In 1848, following the completion of Morley's railway tunnel, the town's first railway station was opened. Due to the high rail fares many people continued to use the horse buses, which plied between Morley, Churwell and Leeds (or they walked). Morleyites, it seems, were reluctant to be 'taken for a ride'. The trams did not arrive at Morley until 1911, although they had been discussed some ten years earlier.

Even the newfangled motorcar did not escape censure. At their meeting on 13 November 1906, the Ardsley (East and West) Urban District Council decided to support the proposals of the Highways Protection League with regard to the regulation of motorcar usage on roads. Councillor Wainwright said, 'If I had my way, no motorcar would be allowed to go more than one mile an hour'. The chairman, who did much motor travelling, replied, 'I think the speed limit is already sufficiently limited'. Councillor Wainwright continued, 'You can't go on the road now without getting your nice suit or dress spoiled'. Amid laughter, the chairman commented, 'I can see I had better leave this subject alone'.

One
Morley and Churwell

Queen Street, Morley, in 1903. This was a time when horse transport prevailed, before tram track was laid. The town hall (with clock) dominates the scene, while Morley Co-op (with cupola) stands on the opposite side of the road.

Queen Street, Morley.

Queen Street, in 1918. Harry Mather's hairdressing salon is shown at No. 72, left of centre. His establishment also served as a tramway parcels office. The tramcar indicator shows Meanwood. This was a through route, via Leeds.

Queen Street, in 1938. The Picture House advertises a film starring the inimitable Lancashire comedian, George Formby.

Queen Street, showing the town hall and
Morley House, to the right. The latter was
demolished, in the 1930s, to make way for
an extension to Scatcherd Park.

Town hall, Morley, in 1904. The memorial
stone was laid, on 8 October 1892, by the
Mayor of Morley, Alderman T. Clough.
The building was opened on 16 October
1895 by the Rt Hon H.H. Asquith MP, the
Morley born politician, who was Home
Secretary at the time.

Town hall, *c.* 1912. The design, by Mr G.A. Fox of the Dewsbury firm of architects, Holtom & Fox, was inspired by Leeds town hall, although it more closely resembles Bolton town hall. The staircase from the pavement leads to a portico of six columns, topped by a pediment. The clock, which was made by Potts & Son, Leeds, was started on 20 April 1895.

Queen Street and town hall, in the 1920s. At No. 62A is the butcher shop of Albert Webster. Over the years, the town hall has accommodated municipal offices, the mayor's reception room and the Borough Court. The two large public halls, named Alexandra Hall and King's Hall, have been used as venues for dramatic performances, orchestral concerts, flower shows and a variety of exhibitions.

Shopping Centre, Morley 7727

Central premises of Morley Industrial Co-operative Society Ltd, c. 1937. Erected at the corner of Morley's Queen Street and Albion Street, they were opened on 8 April 1899. The initial meeting, to form a society in Morley, was held in February 1866. The first store, also in Albion Street, was opened in 1869. In the period up to 1905, around sixteen branch stores were opened, not just in various parts of Morley, but in Gildersome, Tingley, East Ardsley and Thorpe. During this time, further expansion came with the construction of warehouses, stables, a slaughterhouse and bakery. Through bulk buying and the sale of co-op branded goods, the co-operative movement, with its profit sharing dividend, was an attractive choice for working-class people. Morley's original metallic check system was replaced by paper check systems. Bringing out the checks to tot up the divi was a pleasurable pastime! Throughout its existence, Morley Co-op played an active part in the life of the town and beyond. In 1926, a grant of five guineas was made to Morley Brass Band for new instruments. In 1928, twenty guineas were allocated for relief of distress in the South Wales coalfield. A grant of £100 was made to Leeds General Infirmary in 1934, following a special appeal. The central premises, and all the branches of Morley Co-operative Society, have closed, although some of the buildings remain.

In the early 1800s, Morley's two thousand inhabitants lived in several straggling settlements. The greatest concentration was in the Troy Hill/Morley Bottoms area, with its ancient chapel, tiny school, Fleece Inn and windmill for grinding corn. Many of the houses probably contained at least one loom for weaving cloth, either on commission, or for marketing oneself. A beck, now largely culverted, stimulated the building of mills, which needed water for power and various processes. The town grew steadily southwards from the Bottoms via Scatcherd Hill and Queen Street, culminating in the construction of the town hall and various Co-op buildings. Developments to the east and west of Queen Street also proceeded apace. Around 1900, some of the shops at Morley Bottoms were rebuilt. Thus, many of Morley's retail outlets were concentrated at the Bottoms or along Queen Street. Here we can see part of Morley Bottoms, with the beginning of Chapel Hill on the right, early this century. The row of four shops had recently been erected. To the right of Charnock's grocery shop is a branch of the Refuge Assurance Company. Facing south and catching the sun, Lightfoots, left, were making sure their drapery did not fade. Notice the Leeds Empire advert - another attempt to draw people into Leeds!

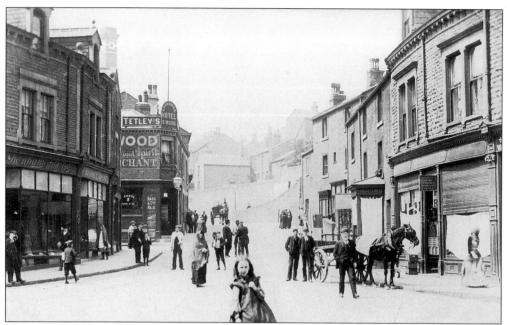

Brunswick Street, in Morley, from the Bottoms, 1904. This lively scene includes Denham & Co., tailors, on extreme left, and Walter Clegg, grocer, extreme right. A sign beside the door indicates that this shop also accepted parcels on behalf of the Great Northern Railway.

Lower end of Queen Street, commonly known as Scatcherd Hill, in 1904. Beyond the well presented drapery establishment is a newsagent's shop with a showy display. Characteristic milltown apparel, such as shawls, cloth caps and clogs is much in evidence in this and the previous view.

Scatcherd Hill, looking towards Cheapside, *c.* 1924. Framed by an ornate tram standard, tramcar No. 247 proceeds in the direction of Leeds. The buildings on the left, dating from the 1840s, were demolished in 1966 for road widening.

Scatcherd Hill. The old part of Morley, before road widening, looks almost idyllic in this *c.* 1965 view.

Queen Street, in the late 1930s. Scatcherd Park is on the right. The buildings on the left date back to the second half of the nineteenth century, a time when the town was expanding southwards.

Queen Street, Morley, *c.* 1912. The above area became the civic and commercial centre of the town. From left to right are the town hall (partly obscured), Lloyds Bank and Morley Co-op, opened respectively in 1895, 1891 and 1899. Behind the trees, on the right, stood the old Manor House.

Manor House, Queen Street. Believed to be over three hundred years old, the house was demolished in the 1930s. It was the birthplace, in 1803, of Sir Titus Salt, the textile magnate who built Saltaire mill and village.

Queen Street, *c.* 1957. Traffic had not yet become too much of a problem and the buses for Leeds still stopped outside the town hall.

Queen Street, *c.* 1963. The newer-looking buildings were erected just before the Second World War. The block on the right, occupied in part by the Yorkshire Electricity Board, had been a Montague Burton tailoring store. The town hall has its new dome, which had been replaced after the fire of 1961.

Christmas greetings from Morley. The card was posted by Percy Sykes (who is described later in the book) to Luneburg, Germany, on 20 December 1909, bearing the message, 'We had a very heavy fall of snow yesterday, about eight inches.'

Bruntcliffe Lane, looking towards Morley Cemetery, in 1903. The bridge, erected in 1857 but since demolished, used to carry the Great Northern Railway line to Gildersome.

South Queen Street, Morley, photographed from Queen Street, in 1950. The Pavilion Cinema later became a bingo hall. The Gallons grocery shop, at the corner with Fountain Street, has a 'best points value' poster in an upper window, which refers to post-war rationing. Butter, cheese, sugar, tea, meat, eggs and sweets still needed points coupons in 1950. Bread and jam had been derationed in 1948.

View from South Queen Street, 1909. In the far distance are houses on King Street. The picture was taken by Percy Sykes, from his photographic studio in South Queen Street. The scene is little changed today, though the setts in the road and the gateway to the churchyard of St Paul's have gone.

Winter scene on Chapel Hill, Morley, looking towards the Bottoms, probably in 1905. The pavement has been cleared, up to the gate of the burial ground, left. The walls and most of the buildings shown are still extant, although the nearest block on the right has been demolished.

New Bank Street, Morley, c. 1905. Here we are looking towards the top of Chapel Hill. Much of New Bank Street was of late nineteenth century development, although most of the buildings pictured here are of earlier vintage. Newer dwellings are visible at the extreme left and right. These later houses, which extended further down New Bank Street, were quite stylish, but of back to back type, in blocks of four to eight, with outside privies across their rear yards.

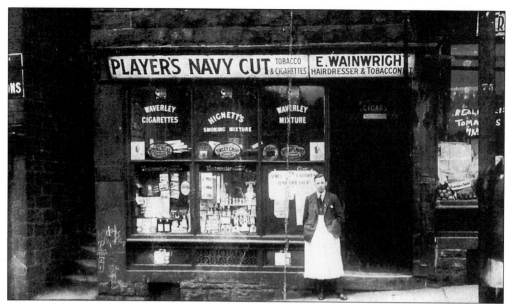

Edgar Wainwright's shop at 31 Queen Street, Morley, in 1927. He was a hairdresser and tobacconist. The steps survive as does the shop, but under a different tenancy.

View from Morley town hall, looking north, *c.* 1937. St Mary's congregational church stands aloft in the middle distance, while several mill chimneys and the spire of St Peter's parish church pierce the skyline.

Public Baths, in Fountain Street, Morley, 1904. Opened in 1900, these included two swimming baths, four vapour baths, twelve slipper baths and a fully equipped laundry. In the mid-1930s, unemployed people were charged 2d each for using the baths. When new swimming baths were opened at Scatcherd Sports Centre, in 1974, the old buildings were demolished.

827   Public Library, Morley.

Public Library, in Commercial Street, Morley, c. 1908. It was built through the beneficence of Andrew Carnegie. The opening ceremony was performed by Hall Caine, the author, on Saturday 27 October 1906. Due to financial constraints, the town council was initially only able to provide 7,886 books.

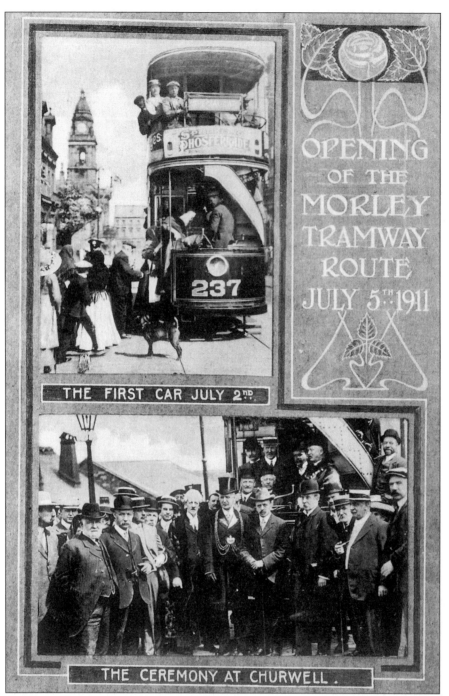

OPENING
OF THE
MORLEY
TRAMWAY
ROUTE
JULY 5TH 1911

THE FIRST CAR JULY 2ND.

THE CEREMONY AT CHURWELL.

Opening of Morley tramway, 1911. Leeds Corporation trams reached Churwell by 1904. Tracks for the extension into Morley were laid in 1911. The first tramcar, No. 237, is seen arriving in Morley during its trial run on Sunday 2 July 1911 (upper picture). The line was officially opened on Wednesday 5 July 1911 with car No. 238, which left Leeds shortly after 11.00a.m. On reaching the foot of Churwell Hill, the Mayor of Morley, Alderman Samuel Rhodes, took over the controls. He is shown in top hat (lower picture).

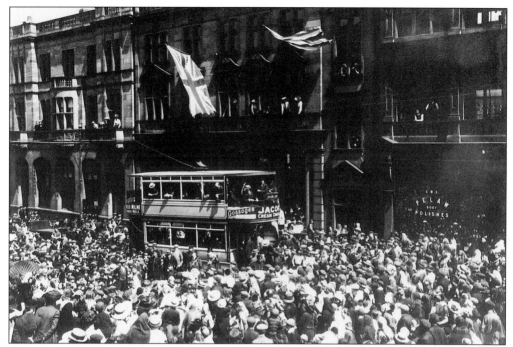

Opening of Morley tramway. With Morley Co-op in the background, tram No. 238 arrives outside Morley town hall on 5 July 1911. A limited passenger service was operated in the afternoon.

Opening of Morley tramway. During the evening of 5 July, a huge gathering of people in Queen Street witnessed the arrival of the Leeds illuminated tram, which had been decorated a few weeks earlier for the coronation of King George V. A full passenger service began on the following day. Morley Corporation owned the tracks within its boundary, which it leased to Leeds Corporation.

MORLEY ST. PETERS SCHOOL, WINNERS OF THE SCATCHERD SHIELD 1900 & 1905

Until the passing of the Forster Education Act of 1870, which made elementary education compulsory for all children between the ages of five and thirteen, schooling in and around Morley, as elsewhere, was fragmented. Various agencies, including religious bodies, voluntarily opened schools in the town. For those unable to take advantage of day school instruction, evening classes were initiated. To carry through the 1870 Education Act, School Boards were formed at Churwell in 1873 and Morley in 1879. Peel Street and Cross Hall Schools were soon built, opening in 1880 and 1881 respectively. Due to a steadily increasing population, further schools were erected and opened in Bridge Street and Victoria Road, in 1896 and 1900. The Balfour Education Act of 1902 made local government responsible for education, with the board schools becoming council schools. A few of the earlier schools, such as St Peter's Church of England School, continued to exist outside council jurisdiction. Some of its sporting pupils are shown above in 1905, having won the Scatcherd Challenge Shield, centre, for the second time. This trophy was inaugurated, in 1900, by Oliver Scatcherd. It was to be competed for by pupils in the town's elementary schools. The contests were in running, long and high jumping, throwing the cricket ball and tug-of-war.

Morley Secondary School, *c.* 1914. Although some provision had been made in Morley for technical education, the West Riding County Council repeatedly stressed the need for the town to provide a purpose-built secondary and technical school. Land was eventually set aside in Fountain Street for a new building. The school, for children of parents residing in Morley, East Ardsley, West Ardsley, Gildersome and Drighlington, was opened on 4 July 1909. Accommodation included a central hall, seven classrooms, a library, gymnasium, chemical and domestic laboratories. The technical section contained textile, engineering and art rooms. The four-acre site allowed for ample playing fields to the front and rear of the main building. The name was eventually changed to Morley Grammar School.

Grammar School, Morley, *c.* 1950.

Cross Hall, Morley, 1908. Dating back to Queen Anne's reign, the house, with its grounds and orchards, was owned by Miss Mary Bosanquet from 1770 to 1782. She converted it into a home for poor and orphaned girls.

Old Rose Cottage, Victoria Road, Morley, *c.* 1905.

The Lodge and St Peter's church, Morley, *c.* 1905. Rooms Lane runs between the two, amongst the trees. The Lodge was demolished and housing now covers most of the field in the foreground.

Rooms Lane, Morley, *c.* 1905. It is viewed from near St Peter's church, looking north. The children in the distance are playing cricket.

Rooms Lane, Morley, *c.* 1920, showing Hughenden and its gatehouse. The M621 was constructed just over the brow of the hill.

Scatcherd Park and Morley Hall, c. 1914. The park is in the foreground. Morley Hall, top right, was built in 1863 and later enlarged. In 1917, Sir Charles Scarth bought the site for the townsfolk. The hall became a maternity home, while the grounds on the hillside became Scarth's Park. To the left of the hall is an old handloom weaving mill.

Scatcherd Park, Morley, c. 1914. The grounds were bequeathed to the town in the will of Oliver Scatcherd. Laid out with paths and flowerbeds, the park was opened to the public on 8 July 1911. It was extended northwards in 1939.

Bridge and lake, Scatcherd Park, *c.* 1922. Queen Street is in the background. Borough accounts, for the twelve months ending 31 March 1937, record that expenditure on Scatcherd Park was £238 1 s 8d. This included £165 16s 9d in wages, £30 7s 1d on repairs and painting, £7 18s 6d on trees, shrubs and seeds, and £11 12s for manure.

Dartmouth Park, *c.* 1912. Situated on the western side of Morley, it was the first of the town's parks to be opened. The land was presented by the Earl of Dartmouth and laid out by the corporation. The earl opened the park on 24 May 1890, this being one of his last public acts, as he died on 4 August 1891.

Elland Road, Churwell, looking towards Morley, *c.* 1904. The steep slope of the road, known locally as Churwell Hill, is apparent. The Old Golden Fleece Inn is only partly visible to the left. The area on the right used to accommodate the village pump.

Elland Road, Churwell, *c.* 1914, looking down towards the area shown on the previous view. The tramway, from the bottom of Churwell Hill into Morley, was mostly single track with passing loops, one of which is shown here.

War Memorial, Churwell. A metal and glass shelter, set in a small garden, is shown fronted by the name plaque. The unveiling was performed on 12 April 1924 by the vicar of Morley, Revd C.J. Barton.

Elland Road, Churwell, in the 1950s. The sign for the Old Golden Fleece Inn and Leeds' famous Melbourne Ales is on the right. To the left, on part of Pump Hill, is the War Memorial.

The College, Churwell, *c.* 1905. It was closed when alternative provision was made in Morley, at first in temporary premises in Commercial Street, and then in the new Morley Secondary School in Fountain Street, which opened in 1909. The old building at Churwell, also known as Morley Grange, became the home of William Law Ingle.

Wellfield House, viewed from Victoria Road, Churwell, in 1905. For many years, it belonged to the Scarth family, whose Laneside Mills were nearby.

A 1935 advertisement.

Two
Drighlington
and Gildersome

King Street, Drighlington, *c.* 1930. The view is seen from the end of Moorside Road, left. Several farms were sited on land to the right of the picture.

Whitehall Road East, Drighlington, from the crossroads, *c.* 1914. The Spotted Cow Inn is on the left, with adverts on its gable wall for Lloyd's News, Keating's Powder and Great Northern Railway excursions to Lincoln and Skegness.

Whitehall Road East, Drighlington, *c.* 1934. This was taken from almost the same spot as the previous view. Not much has changed in the intervening twenty years, but workmen are laying paving flags outside the gate of the old Board School, right. The buildings above the Spotted Cow, left, have since been demolished, but otherwise the scene is little different today.

Crossroads, Drighlington, c. 1930. The Bradford Corporation tram, having negotiated Bradford Road, stands at its terminus. The route was converted to motorbus operation in 1933. The small benzole display, left, may look incongruous, but petrol pumps were located for many years outside the Victoria Hotel, just off the picture to the left. Up Whitehall Road are the imposing premises of the Drighlington Co-operative Industrial Society, erected in 1886 and today housing a Co-op Food Fair.

Hammond Crescent, in Bradford Road, Drighlington, c. 1938. The council houses are fronted by well kept gardens.

Tempest Constitutional Club, in Bradford Road, Drighlington. The club was opened on 4 June 1910. The committee members are grouped at the rear of the building shortly after the opening.

Tempest Constitutional Club. Wives and others are assembled on the same date and location as the top picture. Just look at those hats!

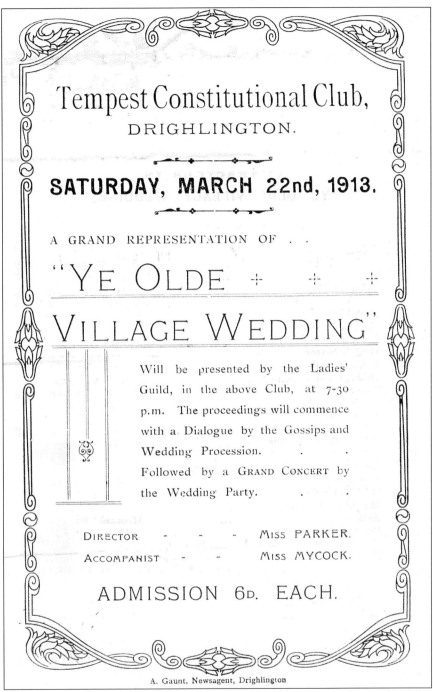

Tempest Constitutional Club,

DRIGHLINGTON.

SATURDAY, MARCH 22nd, 1913.

A GRAND REPRESENTATION OF . .

"YE OLDE ÷ ÷ ÷

VILLAGE WEDDING"

Will be presented by the Ladies' Guild, in the above Club, at 7-30 p.m. The proceedings will commence with a Dialogue by the Gossips and Wedding Procession.

Followed by a GRAND CONCERT by the Wedding Party.

DIRECTOR - - - MISS PARKER.

ACCOMPANIST - - MISS MYCOCK.

ADMISSION 6D. EACH.

A. Gaunt, Newsagent, Drighlington

'Ye Olde Village Wedding' presented at the Tempest Constitutional Club. The inside of the programme (the front cover of which is shown above) lists characters such as bridesmaids, best man, parson, policeman, sailor, schoolmistress and squire. The all female cast included Mrs F. Thompson as the bride and Miss V. Brown as the bridegroom. Also listed are the recitations and songs performed by the ladies, including 'Sweet Genevieve' and 'Little Brown Jug'.

Lumb Bottom, Drighlington, looking towards Nethertown, *c.* 1910. On the left is the Congregational chapel, erected in 1868 to seat three hundred people, but now demolished.

Wyre Hall, Bradford Road, Adwalton, Drighlington, *c.* 1914. Dating from around 1800, it was once occupied by the Moravian Brethren of nearby Fulneck.

Cockersdale, near Gildersome, *c.* 1906. The valley and village, part of which are shown here, both bear the name Cockersdale. The area was mined in the last century for coal, iron ore and fireclay. Power, for its earlier textile mills, was provided by the water of the beck.

The Bottoms, Gildersome, with Harthill in the background, *c.* 1932. Mount Zion chapel is on the right. Very few of the buildings shown here are still extant.

Town Street, Gildersome, from Church Corner, *c.* 1908. Highfield Woollen Mill is in the far distance, with chimney and water tower. New housing now occupies much of the area shown.

Town Street, from near the end of Church Corner, *c.* 1905. The strong presence of children may have been due to the proximity of the Church School.

The Green and Town Street, Gildersome, c. 1905. The Junction Inn and Finkle Lane are on the left. The parish church of St Peter is visible along Church Street, on the right. It has been replaced by a modern building.

Branch Road from the end of Town Street, Gildersome, c. 1904. The right hand shop had been a fruiterers but, at that time, appeared to be selling objects d'art. All the buildings shown have been demolished, but the nearby old Griffin Head Inn (not shown) remains.

Street Lane, Gildersome, looking south, *c.* 1905.

Street Lane, *c.* 1930. It is the same section of road as that in the previous view, but looking in the opposite direction. Little had changed in the intervening quarter of a century. Even today, this part of the lane has hardly altered.

The Vicarage, in Street Lane, *c.* 1905. It is now a home for elderly people. Street Lane School is partly visible, on the left.

Scott Green, Gildersome, looking towards Church Street, *c.* 1932. The houses had recently been constructed.

Church School, in Church Street, Gildersome, *c.* 1905. The school opened in 1897. The high pitched roofs are typical of many Victorian schools. Following fire damage by vandals in 1980, most of the school buildings were demolished.

Street Lane School, Gildersome, *c.* 1906. This was built as a Board School in the 1870s. One of the knickerbockered boys in standard V seems to have borrowed his father's albert!

Three
West Ardsley
and Tingley

The Old Water Mill, Batley Rd.

E. Broadhead. Syke Lane.

Batley Road, *c.* 1923, looking west from near the bottom of Baghill Road. The steam driven mill, centre, had earlier been a water-propelled mill. It was used to grind corn.

Windmill, *c.* 1907. Situated to the west of the Haigh Moor Road, almost opposite Boyle Hall, the windmill remained intact until about 1913.

Thorpe Lane.

J. Tomlinsᵉ
Tingley P

The civil parish of West Ardsley included Tingley, Blackgates, Westerton, Woodkirk, Lee Fair and Haigh Moor. West Ardsley developed mainly as a region of farms and quarries. Tingley crossroads originated as a convergence of the Leeds to Dewsbury and Bradford to Wakefield roads. The crossroads expanded into a huge roundabout, which now incorporates the Lancashire to Yorkshire motorway and its access roads. The 1997 reconstruction has considerably eased the traffic flow. The price of progress was the loss of interesting buildings. The Old White Bear Inn had been built a short distance from the original crossroads, at the end of Thorpe Lane. It is seen on the left of the above picture, *c.* 1925. Thorpe Lane is in the centre. At the opposite side is Joseph Armitage's fried fish shop. All the buildings shown were demolished during the 1967-71 roundabout construction.

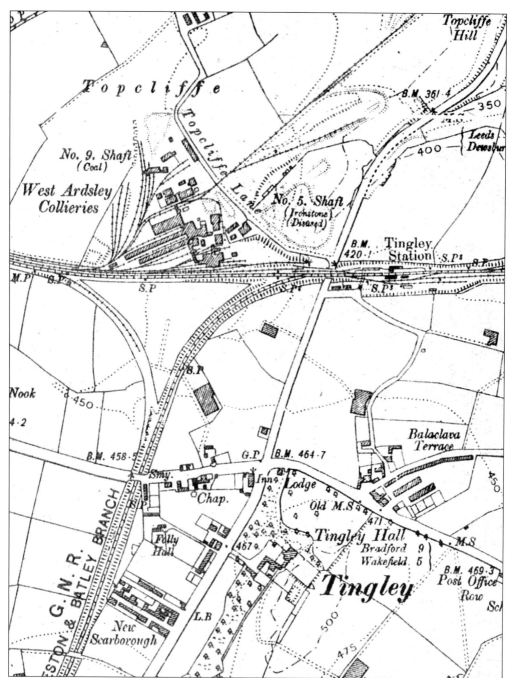

Tingley. This 1919 map (extracted from the *Batley Corporation Jubilee Handbook*) shows a part of Tingley, which has since changed almost beyond recognition. The Bradford to Wakefield road runs left to right. Marked on the map, near the crossroads, are the New White Bear Inn and Tingley Hall. The Old White Bear Inn is to the right, near Balaclava Terrace, although not actually named. The now vanished Topcliffe (West Ardsley) Colliery and Tingley Station are depicted further to the north. Much of the area between the crossroads and railway station is now taken up by the huge road roundabout.

New White Bear Inn, Tingley, *c.* 1934. Built adjacent to the old crossroads, this inn still remains, albeit much altered and with a different name. To the left is the Lodge of Tingley Hall, built in the early eighteenth century. These buildings were demolished in 1967 in connection with road development.

TINGLEY TRAM TERMINUS, MORLEY.

Tingley Mills, *c.* 1924. The tramway to Morley was extended to this point - appropriately named because of its textile mills. The official opening was on 21 October 1911. An extension from Morley to Bruntcliffe opened on 1 January 1912. All the routes through Morley were cut back to the Leeds boundary on 22 January 1935.

Bradford Road, Blackgates, *c*. 1912. Blackgates formerly consisted of these houses plus others, on a series of streets stretching north from here. Much new house building has taken place in the area, particularly to the south.

Bradford Road, Blackgates, *c*. 1925, looking towards Tingley Crossroads. This shows the aspect westwards from the previous view. Visible on the left is the bell tower of Blackgates Board School, erected in 1894-6 to house 450 pupils.

Batley Co-operative Society, branch No. 2, *c.* 1914. Co-operative societies tended to encroach on each others territories. The Batley society built this shop in Westerton Road, West Ardsley in 1874, to replace its short-lived shops at Beggarington and Upper Green.

Batley Co-op, branch No. 11, Hill Top, in West Ardsley, *c.* 1914. Having established branches at Westerton and Tingley, a third (temporary) shop was opened at Hill Top in 1891. After an eighteen month trial period, when success seemed assured, it was replaced by a newly-built store, shown opposite. Thus, the West Ardsley area acquired three Batley Co-op stores.

040 Lee Fair.

Westerton Road, West Ardsley, from the Lee Fair end, in 1908. At the roadside, in the distance, is the original British Oak Tavern, with Westerton School to its left. Slightly nearer, under construction, is the Methodist Sunday School. The nearest building in the distant row is the Co-op, shown in close-up at the top of the previous page. The activity on the above picture could have been in connection with the famous Lee Fair or Lee Gap Fair, although the actual event is not shown. The ancient annual fair was originally called Woodkirk Fair. It is commemorated in a stained glass window in Woodkirk church. Lee Fair would, at one time, last for three weeks, but was curtailed to the first and last days of the original period, that is 24 August and 17 September. These became known as First Lee and Latter Lee. Cloth, hides, pots and cheeses were traded, as well as livestock. Sideshows, boxing booths, sports and a strong gypsy presence added to the atmosphere of the fair, which was renowned for revelry, drinking and fisticuffs. The fair, held at the fairground off Baghill Road, has survived to the present day. However, its activities have become mainly confined to trading in horses, ponies and equestrian equipment.

Four
East Ardsley

Bradford Road, East Ardsley, *c.* 1925. The old forge, left, then belonged to Charlie Stansfield. The drapery shop of Hedley George Stokes is on the right, with the post office, which he managed from about 1925, next door. The light-coloured building, with a gable end facing the road, housed a branch of the Midland Bank (open 10.30a.m. to 1.00p.m, Monday and Friday).

Bradford Road, East Ardsley, in the early 1920s. This view looks towards Thomas Ambler's Mill.

Bradford Road, mid-1930s. Although photographed from a similar spot to the previous picture, the many new houses have created quite a transformation.

Main Street, East Ardsley, *c.* 1906. The terraced houses on the left have spacious gardens (with clothes posts). The long terrace, known as Grand View, was demolished to make way for new housing. On the right is East Ardsley Old Hall, dating from 1622.

Main Street, East Ardsley, *c.* 1906, looking towards the Bedford Arms in the centre distance. On the right is Tom Schofield's grocery shop. Some of the buildings, being at or below road level, were susceptible to flooding during heavy rain. As a result of demolition, the overall scene looks much different today.

The Falls, East Ardsley. Maps usually referred to the area as the Fall, but local people generally called it the Falls. The close-knit, self-contained community consisted of streets of terraced houses, mostly of the back to back type, and a few shops. No. 4 Jackson's View was fairly typical and is pictured here in 1908. It has sash windows, roll-up blinds, as well as curtains, and a fanlight over the door for extra light. At the time, any locally posted letters or cards received 'The Fall' postmark.

Advertisements from the November 1911 issue of East Ardsley parish magazine.

Bradford Road, in East Ardsley, looking towards the end of Main Street, *c.* 1925.

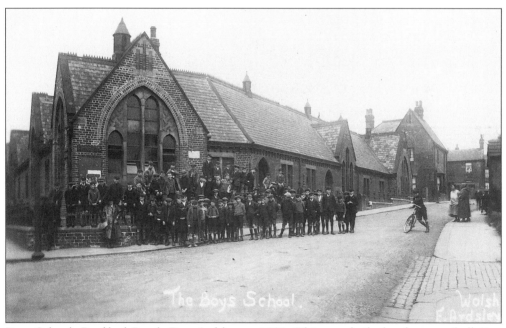

Boys School, Bradford Road, East Ardsley, *c.* 1923. This was built for the use of all East Ardsley's school children in 1874, but the girls and infants were transferred to a new school, in Fall Lane, in 1892. After becoming redundant, the original school building was reopened as a youth club, by former pupil Ernie Wise, in 1967. The building has recently been demolished.

Stanhope Grove, Thorpe, *c.* 1907. The village of Thorpe was situated just outside Morley borough boundary and was physically separated from East Ardsley by a beck and the railway. Thorpe was partly developed as a village for the housing of local railway workers. The above terrace was nicknamed 'Pretty Window Row' because of the stylish bays.

Thorpe School, Dolphin Lane. Shown here in new condition, the school was erected in 1907 to take 260 children.

Five
Churches and Chapels

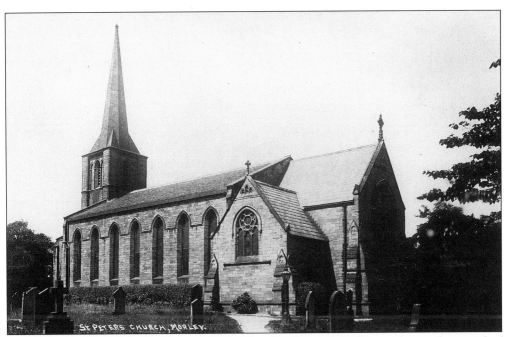

St Peter's parish church, Morley, in 1905. The church is situated near the northern end of Church Street, in the older part of Morley. It was built in 1829-30 with financial help from the government and Lord Dartmouth.

Morley Old Chapel, Commercial Street. The engraving shows the building prior to the alterations of the early 1860s. It was demolished in 1875. The nave may have dated back to 1560, the chancel to 1100. The building's history was chequered by the various struggles between the dissenting Puritans and the Established Church. The former wished to purify the latter of much of the ceremonial. In 1693, the chapel was handed back to the dissenters. A period of stagnation was reversed by a succession of forceful ministers and preachers, mainly of Congregational persuasion. Although the 1860s alterations were made in an attempt to modernise the building, it was deemed unsafe in 1875 and pulled down. St Mary's Congregational church was erected on the same site and opened on 5 September 1878. Since then, it has remained a landmark near the centre of the town.

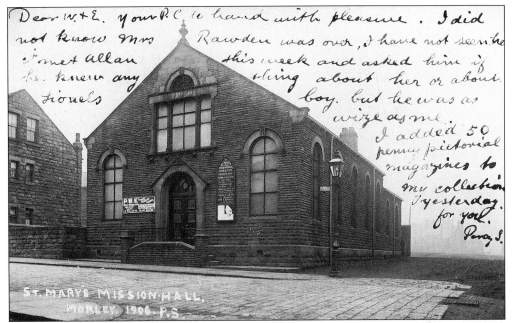

Dear W.+E. Your P.C to hand with pleasure. I did not know Mrs Rawden was over, I have not seen her. I met Allan this week and asked him if he knew anything about her or about Lionels boy. but he was as wise as me. I added 50 penny pictorial magazines to my collection yesterday. for you. Percy S.

ST. MARY'S MISSION HALL. MORLEY. 1906. P.S

St Mary's Congregational Mission Hall, Middleton Road, Morley, in 1906. This chapel was erected in 1889 to meet the needs of a working class area, to the east of the town centre, and was served by a series of evangelists. The PWE (Pleasant Wednesday Evening) meetings were an attempt to reach outsiders. Photographer Percy Sykes, who produced the postcard, couldn't resist the temptation to write his message across the sky.

Baptist Tabernacle, Commercial Street, Morley, c. 1905. It was built in Renaissance style, in 1896, to seat 600 people, from a design by architects Hanstock & Co., of Batley. The older chapel facing Albion Street, right, became the Sunday school.

John Wesley, founder of Methodism, preached in Morley several times from 1747 onwards, mostly in the open air or in private houses. Hospitality was eventually provided by Miss Mary Bosanquet at her residence, Cross Hall. Partly through this lady's enterprise, Methodism became established in Morley. Countrywide, the original Wesleyan Methodist body, which was a breakaway from the Church of England, itself became subject to various secessions. By 1907, some consolidation had taken place, the three main branches becoming the Wesleyan, Primitive and United Methodist churches. The profusion of Methodist buildings in and around Morley was a measure of the zeal of the various branches (and often the benevolence of wealthy manufacturers). To these must be added the buildings of the similarly fervent Baptists and Congregationalists. In 1932, Methodist Union brought together the various Methodist groups. However, the once thriving edifices became a liability from the 1950s onwards. The Wesleyan chapel, off Queen Street, Morley, is shown above, *c.* 1905. Replacing a 1770 structure, it was built in 1859-61, with a continuous oval gallery inside and box pews at both levels. After absorbing the congregations of other Methodist chapels in the town, which had closed, it became known as Central Methodist.

Wesleyan Sunday School, Queen Street, *c.* 1910. This was built in 1883-4. The chapel is visible to the rear. The schoolroom was demolished in 1968 and a smaller one was erected behind the chapel.

Cross Hall Wesleyan chapel, Bruntcliffe Road, Morley, *c.* 1903. It was erected in 1878-9 near to the junction with Fountain Street. Observe the letter box in the wall on the left.

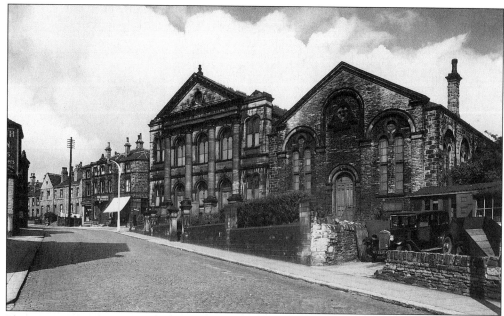

Ebenezer Methodist chapel, Fountain Street, in Morley, *c.* 1937. This was Primitive Methodist up to 1932. The left hand side building was opened on 30 September 1886, with a seating capacity of 1,050, including the gallery. The earlier building, right, dating from 1878, continued in use as a Sunday school.

Harvest Festival at Morley Ebenezer, October 1910.

Roman Catholic church of St Francis of Assisi, in Corporation Street, Morley, *c*. 1905.

Temperance Hall, in Fountain Street, Morley. The interior appears to be laid out for some special event, possibly the reopening celebrations of September 1905, after painting, decorating and installation of new lighting. On that occasion, the hall was adorned with plants and flowers and an excellent tea was provided by the ladies (note the tea tables). Special services were also held.

Stone laying ceremony, Salvation Army Barracks, in Ackroyd Street, Morley, 6 April 1907.
Members and friends had assembled outside the old barracks in Albion Street. Accompanied by
Salvation Army bands from Morley and other areas, they marched to Ackroyd Street. Above,
in the presence of the mayor, Alderman S. Rhodes, the opening hymn, 'Jesus the name high
over all', is being announced. After the ceremony, a substantial tea was served in the old
headquarters.

St Mary's parish church, Woodkirk, in 1904. Part of the unbuttressed tower dates from the
thirteenth century, but the rest of the church was rebuilt after storm damage in 1831.

St Michael's. E. Ardsley.

St Michael's parish church, East Ardsley, c. 1910. Built on the site of a much earlier church, it was consecrated in 1881. The Revd John H.D. Hill arrived as vicar of the old St Michael's in 1875. He instigated the building of a Sunday school in 1878, the new St Michael's in 1881 and St Gabriel's church on Fall Lane in 1889. The hardworking vicar refused better posts and remained in the village until his death in 1928. The outspoken cleric pulled no punches. In his parish magazine of January 1910, he rebuked part of his flock for their absence at Sunday morning services, 'I know I ought to take into consideration the fact that most of our worshippers are six-day workers, and that many of them have to rise at five o'clock to go to their work, but I do not forget that most of them leave work on Saturdays at midday; and I can't help thinking that they might retire early enough on Saturday nights to secure a good night's rest and yet be in time to attend the 10.30 service; whereas too many of them wear themselves out with pleasure, and lay the blame on the six days' early rising instead of the late Saturday night revelling.' In the August issue, the vicar wrote about the irreverent behaviour of women and children who frequented the churchyard at the time of funerals, 'They come, often an hour before the funeral, and spend the time in idle gossip, and when the funeral procession enters the churchyard and the service is proceeding, they have not the decency to keep their tongues quiet.' By October, he had switched his attention to hymn books, stating that, in future, worshippers would be expected to bring their own, rather than the church provide them. They could be purchased for 6d each!

St Michael's church, East Ardsley, *c.* 1905. Also shown, bottom right, is St Gabriel's Mission church, built in 1889 for the expanding population in the Falls area. At the bottom left is Fall Lane School, erected in 1892 for girls and infants and enlarged in 1901.

St Paul's Wesleyan Methodist chapel, Chapel Street, East Ardsley, *c.* 1905. This was built in 1889 to replace an earlier building. At the Sunday school prize distribution on Saturday 12 February 1927, the scholars presented a concert of recitations and choral items. However, it was reported that, 'there were not many there to hear the children.' In 1966, after the closure of the two other Methodist chapels in the area (Zion and Bethel), their congregations joined with the people of St Paul's Methodist, which became known as East Ardsley Methodist.

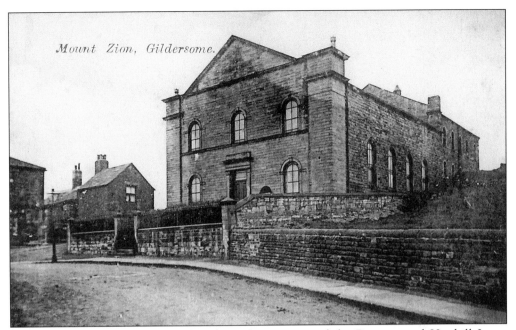

Mount Zion United Methodist chapel, at the junction of the Bottoms and Harthill Lane, Gildersome, *c.* 1907. The chapel has been demolished, but the schoolroom at the rear has survived for alternative use. The congregation now worships at the nearby Greenside Methodist church, formerly a Wesleyan building.

Zion United Methodist chapel, Three Lane Ends, Adwalton, *c.* 1912. From this angle we are looking towards Wakefield Road. The building was erected in 1870 and demolished in 1970.

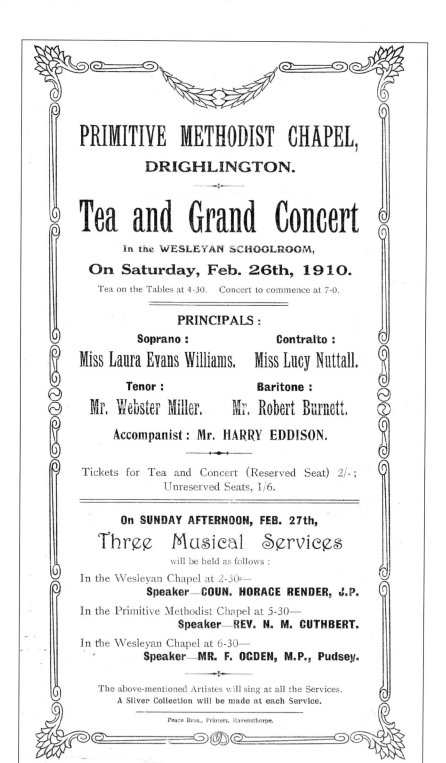

PRIMITIVE METHODIST CHAPEL,

DRIGHLINGTON.

Tea and Grand Concert

In the WESLEYAN SCHOOLROOM,

On Saturday, Feb. 26th, 1910.

Tea on the Tables at 4-30.   Concert to commence at 7-0.

PRINCIPALS :

Soprano :

Contralto :

Miss Laura Evans Williams.   Miss Lucy Nuttall.

Tenor :

Baritone :

Mr. Webster Miller.   Mr. Robert Burnett.

Accompanist : Mr. HARRY EDDISON.

Tickets for Tea and Concert (Reserved Seat) 2/- ;
Unreserved Seats, 1/6.

On SUNDAY AFTERNOON, FEB. 27th,

Three Musical Services

will be held as follows :

In the Wesleyan Chapel at 2-30—
Speaker—COUN. HORACE RENDER, J.P.

In the Primitive Methodist Chapel at 5-30—
Speaker—REV. N. M. CUTHBERT.

In the Wesleyan Chapel at 6-30—
Speaker—MR. F. OGDEN, M.P., Pudsey.

The above-mentioned Artistes will sing at all the Services.
A Silver Collection will be made at each Service.

Peace Bros., Printers, Ravensthorpe.

Tea and Grand Concert at the Primitive Methodist chapel, Drighlington. The front of the programme is illustrated. It shows that there was some cooperation between the Primitives and Wesleyans.

76

Six
Industry and Transport

An early delivery wagon belonging to Morley Industrial Co-operative Society.

CRANK MILLS MORLEY

Crank Mill, in Station Road, Morley, c. 1903. Unlike some towns, Morley, with its elevated position, was not ideally suited for water-powered mills. This resulted in Yorkshire's first steam-powered mill being constructed at Morley in the early 1790s. Erected by the Earl of Dartmouth, but leased to brothers James and Joseph Webster, who were members of an old cloth-making family, it became known as Crank Mill. The engine house contained only the engine cylinder - the crank and flywheel being outside. In the mid-nineteenth century, these were replaced by an enclosed beam engine, in a new engine house. When the mill was first built, handloom weavers brought their wool to it for scribbling and fulling. The complex was later enlarged and became a cloth finishing mill. In the above photograph, Station Road is in the foreground (leading down through the bridge). The smaller of two mill ponds is visible behind the wall on the left (where a man is standing).

Hudson, Sykes & Bousfield Ltd, Springfield Mills, Morley, *c.* 1930. The firm was located at the northern end of Springfield Lane, near the Upper Rooms area of Morley, where they produced woollens and worsteds. The complex was eventually taken over by the Bradford firm of Hield Brothers Ltd.

Wagon builder's and repairer's yard, *c.* 1905. The location is not known, possibly it is carriage builder Robert Webster's premises at Morley's Bank Top. The names on the covered vehicles represent two well known Morley woollen manufacturers; left, J. & S. Rhodes Ltd of Prospect Mills, Bank Street, and Queen Mills, Albion Street; right, John Hartley & Sons Ltd of Gillroyd Mills. The wagons were used for carrying cloth.

Walter B. Stockwell, Alexandra Mills, Morley. The firm's solid-tyred vehicle, used for carrying bales of rags, has a Leeds registration. Described as a rag and mungo merchant, Stockwell's premises were off Fountain Street, and approached via Baker Street. Nearby, there were large rag warehouses owned by the Great Northern Railway. For a time, Stockwell also had premises on High Street.

Mill workers in the Morley area. The youngest girls, on the front row, possibly aged thirteen or under, may have started working as half-timers when they were twelve. In one week, such half-timers would work at the mill in the morning and attend school in the afternoon, the following week, vice-versa. The system was not outlawed until 1922.

Morley Main Colliery, on Albert Road. The drawing, from the *Illustrated London News*, was produced after the explosion of 7 October 1872. Over thirty miners and eleven ponies were killed. Corves, filled with coal, were overturned by the force of the blast. During the inquest, it emerged that some of the men had probably been smoking at the coal face. Many of the miners suffocated, the explosion having cut off the means of ventilation. The colliery, which opened in 1855, was closed in 1909.

Coal delivery cart. Smith's depot, where coal was loaded on to the carts, was near the GNR station. The coal was tipped up at factories and private houses. Many householders had to shovel it through their cellar grates. Then came bagged coal, smokeless fuel and motorised transport. By the 1950s, horse-drawn coal carts had almost disappeared.

Glass blowing at Hailwood and Ackroyd Ltd, Morley, c. 1934.

Hailwood and Ackroyd Ltd, advertisement for 1936. The business commenced as a partnership between William Ackroyd and William Best and was known as Ackroyd & Best Ltd. Best had been a lamp cleaner at Morley Main Colliery. The name was changed to Hailwood & Ackroyd Ltd in 1927, following the appointment of E.A. Hailwood as a manager. The company remained at the forefront of colliery safety lamp manufacture until production ceased around 1960. By then, the firm was also producing light fittings, hydraulic valves and precision engineering parts, some of them for the automative industry.

Morley Sewage Disposal Works, c. 1904. These were laid out behind the Woodman Inn on Dewsbury Road. Their opening in 1901 was a foretoken of Morley Council's intention to gradually replace all dry privies with individual water closets, although it was some time before the plan was completed.

Morley Sewage Disposal Works. Improvements were ongoing, as is shown here by work being carried out by Naylor Brothers of Denby Dale in 1907. A few years later, plant was installed to extract oil from the effluent. The oil was sold to raise income.

Morley Corporation fire brigade, 1904. The equipment of the Morley Mutual Fire Insurance Co. Ltd, founded in 1872 by a consortium of mill owners, was absorbed by the Corporation in 1902. Standing at extreme right, in front of the horse-drawn appliance, is George Albert Firth, who had risen from the rank of fireman to become superintendent. He lived in High Street.

Morley Top Station, High Street, *c.* 1905. Although the London & North Western Railway was first to arrive in the Morley area, the Great Northern Railway exerted more influence. The LNWR's Morley Station opened in 1848; the GNR opened theirs in 1857. To avoid confusion, it was known as Morley Top. It closed in 1961.

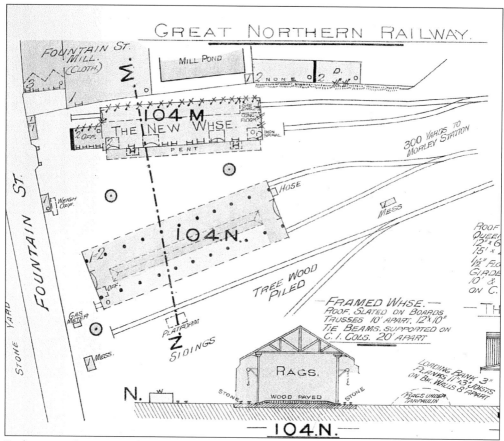

Railway warehouses, Morley. These plans were prepared for insurance purposes in 1896. Rags were brought, by rail, to Morley from London, provincial towns and abroad. They were stored in large warehouses to await disposal (often by auction) for processing at local mills. The GNR warehouses are shown on this page (and partly on the next). The newer GNR warehouse, near Fountain Street Mill, was built with two storeys, in order to cater for increased demand.

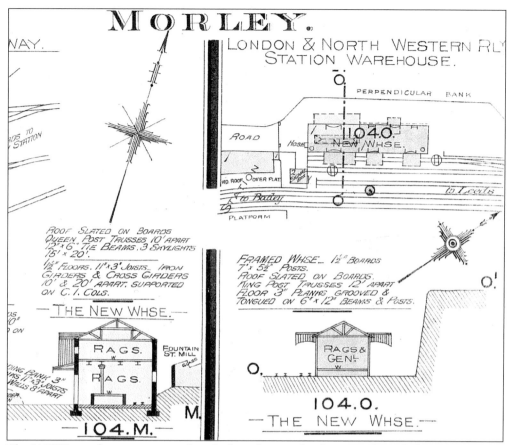

The LNWR warehouse was erected in the lee of a steep bank, as is indicated above.

HENRY BOOTH & SONS

MOOR HEAD MILLS

GILDERSOME : nr. LEEDS : ENGLAND

Partners { ALFRED BOOTH HENRY BOOTH } Grandsons of the Founder.

A portion of the electrically-driven Woollen Spinning Plant.
Installed 1914.

Actual Manufacturers of all classes of Uniform Cloths and Serges, also Superfines, Beavers, Overcoatings, Carriage Cloths, Serges, Worsteds, etc., for Civilian Wear.

Henry Booth & Sons, Moor Head Mills, Gildersome. This advertisement, from 1917, shows part of the firm's 1914 modernisation.

Scott's Mineral Waters, Drighlington. Horse-drawn rulleys, like this, delivered 'pop' to people's homes, usually once a week. The business was founded in the late nineteenth century by Edward Scott. The premises on Whitehall Road, near Drighlington's crossroads, were known as the Crystal Mineral Water Works. The firm became Scott, Simpson & Co. in about 1924. Drighlington's other mineral water concern was Parker Brothers of King Street.

Workers at Packard & Stead Ltd, galvanisers, Drighlington, *c.* 1930.

Gildersome Station, *c.* 1905. This GNR station was opened in 1856. Passenger facilities were withdrawn in 1955, as were goods services in 1965. The view, looking west, shows the track entering the 156 yard long tunnel under Gildersome crossroads. Gildersome's other station, belonging to the LNWR, was opened in 1900 and closed permanently in 1921.

Gildersome GNR station, *c.* 1905, looking east. Apart from the double-gabled station house, the buildings have little architectural merit, although the walls provide plenty of space for posters. The nearby sidings handled coal. Slightly further east were extensive sidings, which connected with Robert Hudson's Gildersome Foundry.

Thomas Ambler & Sons, Bradford Road, East Ardsley. The firm originated in Bradford in 1858. Due to the readily available coal and female labour, Ardsley was chosen as the site for a new worsted spinning mill. Built in 1912-3, it is shown nearing completion.

Ambler's Mill, c. 1922. The mill was built on modern lines, with large windows. Until the 1960s, a giant steam engine provided power.

Ambler's Mill. The changing face of Ambler's transport is portrayed on this 1951 advertisement.

East Ardsley Colliery, from Moor Knoll Lane, *c*. 1912. The shafts were sunk in 1872 by Robert Holliday & Sons. Part of the screening plant, with coal staiths, is shown. Pit props and rail wagons are also visible. The colliery was abandoned in 1968.

Ardsley Station, *c*. 1908. The GNR saw the potential of making Ardsley into a railway centre. Near the five-platform station can be seen the Great Northern Hotel, right. An impressive arrangement of siding was laid out around the station and engine shed. The station, which opened in 1857, was closed to passengers in 1964. Today, few reminders of the railway remain, apart from the main line from Leeds to London.

Ardsley Station, looking towards Leeds. The main station buildings are on the left. People on the road bridge are watching soldiers on strike duty in the 1911-12 period, when a series of countrywide disturbances caused chaos.

Ardsley Sheds, *c.* 1905. GNR's motive power depot and adjoining marshalling yard were developed towards the end of the nineteenth century and, in their heyday, provided employment for about four hundred men. The depot allocation was mostly goods engines. The marshalling yard dealt mainly with coal traffic. The sheds were shut down in 1965.

94

Ardsley Station, 1901. The group includes the stationmaster, station staff, signalmen and guards. It is said that large lumps of coal (cobblings) were sometimes hurled by locomen from engines as they passed near houses at East Ardsley and Thorpe, to be commandeered later by the men's families. Perks of the job!

Railway Ambulance Division, East Ardsley, c. 1917. These men attended classes and lectures, entered examinations and held competitions with other divisions. In February 1939, at a contest at the Trades & Labour Club in Wakefield, Ardsley beat Dewsbury, Bradford Goods and Lofthouse and were presented with a shield.

A. S. L. E. & F.

ARDSLEY BRANCH.

AN

Open Meeting

of

ENGINEMEN. FIREMEN and CLEANERS,

will be held in the

Labour Hall, Fall Lane, East Ardsley,

on

SUNDAY, JULY 23rd, 1933,

to be addressed by

Mr. W. P. ALLEN, of Hornsey,

President of the Society.   Subject :

"The Danger of Apathy to Locomotivemen."

Chair to be taken at 2.30 p.m., by

Mr, L. GILKS.

Questions Invited.

All Locomotivemen off duty are earnestly invited to attend.

Notice of a meeting of the Associated Society of Locomotive Engineers & Firemen, Ardsley branch, in 1933.

GNR 0-6-0 No. 374, at Ardsley Motive Power Depot, in April 1907.

Ardsley Station and Ironworks, c. 1925. The West Yorkshire Iron & Coal Co. opened the works in 1868. Ironstone from West Ardsley's Topcliffe Colliery was worked there initially, until other sources were used. The works closed in the early 1930s.

Ardsley Ironworks, 1904. The ovens in the foreground produced coke, which was used, along with iron ore and limestone, in the blast furnaces. Waste slag from the furnaces was used in road construction.

Furnaces, Ardsley Ironworks, c. 1906. The works were at the centre of the village's industrial complex, which included East Ardsley Colliery, gasworks and slag heaps. Half a mile away were engine sheds, two mills and the Falls area, with its working-class houses. Their gardens were virtually nonexistent, so inhabitants made good use of the allotments.

Explosion at Ardsley Ironworks, 28 August 1908. Two men were killed instantly. Of sixteen seriously injured, three later died. A committee was quickly formed in the village to raise money for the widows, orphans, injured and out-of-work. Almost £300 was raised. This fundraising postcard was printed by Warner Gothard of Barnsley, who specialised in producing disaster cards.

Ardsley Ironworks, in 1917, looking towards Common Lane. Local children, centre, appear to be using the blackened landscape as a playground.

George Armitage & Sons Ltd. Although based at Robin Hood, this company controlled several stone quarries in the Morley and Woodkirk areas - they also made bricks. They had railway sidings near Woodkirk station, and owned at fleet of steam wagons, one of which is shown above. The firm originated in 1824.

George Armitage & Sons Ltd. One of their less sophisticated steam wagons, where the driver had to stand on a small platform at the side.

Seven

Leisure

'Ye Olde Village Wedding', presented by Morley Ebenezer married ladies, c. 1908. This popular money-raising entertainment was relatively easy to produce. Dialogue by village gossips and the 'wedding' procession were generally followed by a concert comprising individual items and the sale of bridal cake.

Morley Charities Carnival, 1907. By the early 1900s, this had become an established annual event. It always began with a procession, which included decorated floats such as the one above.

Morley Charities Carnival, probably in 1906. In that year, the parade was followed by merrymaking in the cricket and football fields. The Queen of Roses was crowned. Maypole dances and drills were performed by children of Cross Hall Council School. These were followed by sports, military demonstrations and a firework display. Splendid weather prevailed.

Morley Charities Carnival. By the 1920s and '30s, when the two groups on this page were photographed, motorised floats had replaced some of the horse-drawn ones. The above vehicle was provided by Morley Co-op.

Morley Charities Carnival. The character at the side of the lorry, holding the collecting box, is covered in Oxo Cubes.

Dartmouth Park, Morley, in 1904. The view from outside the main gateway, at the junction of St Andrew's Avenue and New Street, shows the lodge house, one of the greenhouses and an advertisement for the Bradford Exhibition.

Dartmouth Park, Morley, c. 1907, looking towards St Andrew's Avenue. The park boasted fine flower beds, open spaces, a bandstand and a drinking fountain.

Bandstand and Cosy Corner, in Dartmouth Park. Promenading and listening to the band were popular Edwardian pastimes, especially on a Sunday.

Scatcherd Park, Morley, in August 1911. The view looks towards Co-operative Street. This town centre oasis, with gardens, seating and a bowling green (top left), soon became popular. One of the bylaws issued in 1912 stated, 'A person shall not, in any part of the pleasure ground, hang, spread or deposit any linen for the purpose of drying or bleaching.'

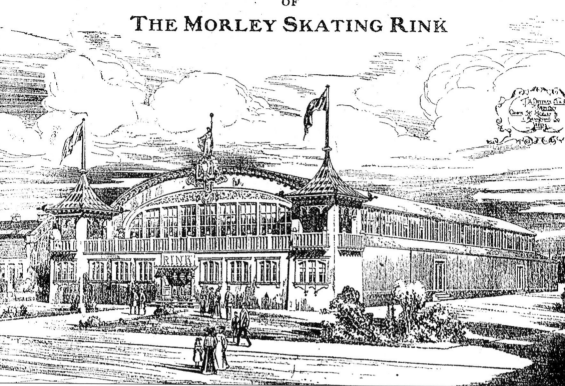

Roller Skating Rink, Oak Road (off Fountain Street), Morley. With its flamboyantly styled frontage, the rink was opened on Wednesday 29 September 1909 at 7p.m. (the launch having been postponed due to wet weather). The above drawing, prepared by the architect, Mr T.A. Buttery of Queen Street, appeared in the *Morley Observer* at the time. The structure had brick/concrete foundations, a steel frame and sides made from wood and corrugated iron. The elaborate façade was fashioned in cemented plaster. Although there was no opening ceremony, several thousand people queued on the first evening to take advantage of the free entry. Very quickly, an estimated 200 to 300 skaters packed the rink, having hired skates at 6d a time. Brooks' Brass Band supplied the music. The rink proved to be very popular. Three sessions per day were held, in the morning, afternoon and evening. Admission was generally 6d, but was free in the morning and also free to ladies in the afternoon. Skates continued to be hired at 6d a time. Friday was usually a special night, when hire of skates would cost one shilling.

Roller Skating Rink, Morley, 1909. The actual rink measured 50 yards by 21 yards. The various facilities included a café.

Morley Low Station during Morley Feast, c. 1903. During this period, which lasted about a week, mill hooters were silent and tea cans were put away. By the 1930s, many families could manage to go away for a week, but the folk above are off on a day excursion to Blackpool. The non-corridor, third-class carriages may have created a problem for those wishing to spend a penny. This station is still open.

Church of Christ Sunday School. Around Whitsuntide, most Sunday schools held anniversaries, parades and school feasts. Whitsun was also a time for wearing new clothes. Morley used to come alive on Whit Monday when each of about a dozen Sunday schools held its own parade through the streets. A few Sunday schools chose an alternative day. Various halts were made to sing special hymns, the town hall steps being a favourite stopping place. Above, in front of the town hall on Whit Monday 1906, are scholars and friends from the Church of Christ as they prepare to sing. Observe the banner with its Bible motif. These children had assembled at their church in the Birks area at 1.30p.m. During their parade, four stops were made for singing. Later, one hundred scholars sat down to tea and, during the evening, enjoyed games and sports in a field.

Co-op Children's Gala, in Drighlington, August 1911. At their quarterly meeting, the Drighlington & District Co-operative Society (formerly the Drighlington Co-operative Industrial Society) decided to give all member's children, between the ages of four and fifteen, a special treat. Their decision was made to celebrate the society's recovery from the financial difficulties, which had beset it six years earlier. On the day, five hundred children assembled for the festivities. With Birstall Brass Band at the front and Drighlington & Adwalton Comic Prize Band at the rear, they, along with officials, parents and uniformed organisations, paraded through the village, via King Street, Moorside, Hodgson Lane and Whitehall road. The procession is shown in Whitehall Road, slightly higher up than the Co-op premises. Returning to Drighlington Park, the children were served with buns and tea. Each child was presented with a commemorative mug and a box of chocolates. After tea, the two bands played. Further entertainment was provided by Monsieur Ducarel with Punch & Judy, conjuring and ventriloquism.

Gala procession, in King Street, Adwalton, looking towards Wakefield Road, *c.* 1906. Melton's drapery shop forms part of the block on the left, which is still there, although the shop has closed. The Mechanics' Institute, in the background, and the houses on each side of it, have since been demolished. Its facilities included evening technical classes and a library.

This bonfire was built to celebrate the coronation of King George V and Queen Mary on Hart Hill, Gildersome, in 1911. An earlier coronation bonfire had been lit there in 1902.

Tyrrell's Berry Gardens, Cockersdale, *c.* 1910. The original fruit gardens were developed into pleasure grounds early this century. The beck was dammed to form a small lake with a pleasure boat. Refreshments were served and a band played at holiday times. Wagonettes brought Sunday school children to the gardens on their annual outings.

Woodkirk Gardens, 1910. Although this piece of Woodkirk was just over the boundary, it was popular with Morley and West Ardsley residents. Apart from the gardens, the grounds included a tea room, dance hall, roundabouts and a zoo. The site later became a housing estate.

Sports Challenge Shield. This was presented by F.B. Hudson of Hudson, Sykes & Bousfield Ltd, Springfield Mills, Morley, in 1903.

Morley Cricket Club, 1912. Morley Nelson and Morley Britannia Cricket Clubs were forerunners of this team, probably photographed at the ground in Scatcherd Lane. This and the adjoining football ground were opened on 5 July 1889.

Ardsley Celtic football team, 1920-21. Seated second from right, on the middle row, is Alvin Woollin, who later resided at Outwood and became a Methodist local preacher.

Messrs Cage and Bricheno. Harp, banjo and vocal items were performed by this pair from the Falls, in East Ardsley.

Eight
People and Events

Primitive Methodist Sunday school group, Churwell. They are pictured on the Tuesday after Easter, in 1908. The girls are wearing crowns and carry posies, each made from spring flowers; the boys have buttonholes of narcissi. The young lady in black, to the right, is Miss Peace. They are pictured in the vicinity of the railway.

Samuel Stead. He commenced business as a printer in 1852 in Morley Bottoms. He moved to premises in Albion Street and later into Troy Road, by which time his sons had entered the concern. In October 1871, Samuel Stead founded the *Morley Observer* and published it every Friday. An 1890s blurb stated, 'It eschews that heavy solid aspect of journalism which is dying out and adopts the new journalistic style of bright, smart, paragraphs which is now becoming so popular.'

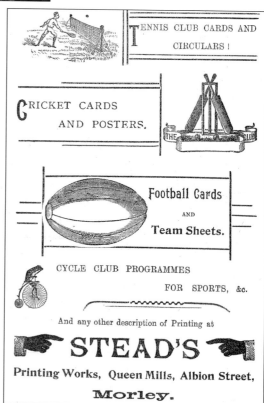

Samuel Stead advertisement, 1894.

Croft House, Church St., Morley. Birthplace of H. H. Asquith, Prime Minister.

Croft House, Church Street, Morley. This was the birthplace of Herbert Henry Asquith (1852-1928) who was Prime Minister from 1908 to 1916. After the death of his father, Herbert (aged seven), moved with the rest of his family to Mirfield. A lawyer by profession, he was elected as a Liberal MP for East Fife in 1886. He later became Home Secretary, Chancellor of the Exchequer, leader of the Liberal Party and Prime Minister.

Morley town hall and parts of the town were lavishly decorated with bunting when the Rt Hon Herbert Henry Asquith came to receive the Freedom of the Borough on 24 July 1913. At the town hall, the Mayor of Morley, Alderman William Law Ingle, presented the Prime Minister with a beautiful casket containing an illuminated manuscript. The picture shows Mr Asquith descending the town hall steps after the ceremony, with Mr Ingle behind and Miss Violet Asquith, his daughter, on the right. The group then attended a garden party at Morley Grange.

The Right Hon. H. H. Asquith, (Prime Minister) leaving the Town Hall, Morley, after recieving the Freedom of the Borough. July 24th 1913.
Photo by A. Webster

Fire at R. & J. Horsfall's Albion Mills, Morley, 15 July 1915. A crowd of several thousand watched Morley and Leeds fire brigades fight the fire, which started at 9 o'clock on Saturday evening. Suddenly a man appeared on the second floor. On being forcibly brought down by two firemen, he said, 'I went up there to see the fire.' Found to be drunk, he was locked up by the police. The inside of the four-storey building was destroyed.

Fire at Allied Mills, Gildersome, 30 August 1911. Mills were fire hazards because of the way they were constructed and the nature of the materials processed. This was at least the second severe fire at Allied.

George Cadd, wife Elizabeth (née Littlewood) and daughter Betty, in 1935. They lived in the Falls area of East Ardsley for many years. George worked on the railway and obtained concessionary travel. This meant that while some other local people holidayed in Blackpool or Scarborough, Mr and Mrs Cadd and Betty were able to go by train to their favourite resort of Great Yarmouth. George's hobby was photography.

An earlier photograph of George Cadd in a dashing suit, which attracted a good deal of ragging from his friends. George was born in 1885 and died in 1943. Elizabeth, who was born in 1887, survived him by nearly ten years.

Morley Technical School, summer surveying class, in 1921. The mixed party await departure

MORLEY TECH! SCHOOL.
SUMMER SURVEYING CLASS · 192

outside the fire station, behind the town hall.

121

Photographic studio of Percy Sykes, South Queen Street, Morley. A lot of the pictures in this book are taken from photographs that appeared on postcards. Early this century, several notable photographers worked in Morley. One of the most prolific was R. Simpson, who had a studio opposite St Peter's church in Victoria Road. Simpson sold his studio in 1908 and took over a public house near Huddersfield. Equally popular was Dan Wilkinson, whose postcards were sold in A. Wilkinson's newsagency and stationery shop at the Bottoms. Tom Stevenson worked from a studio in South Queen Street. Although these unsung artists produced family portraits, they are perhaps better remembered today for recording the everyday life of Morley - street scenes, transport, events, disasters and the like. Some of the images may have faded because the photographers were too busy to allow time for the various photographic chemicals to work properly. Also operating from South Queen Street was Percy Sykes. His photographic studio, on the east side of the street, almost opposite St Paul's church, is shown above, left. The decorations are part of Carnival Day, 27 June 1908. Percy, having taken shots of the carnival procession, decided to take one of his studio.

Percy Sykes in 1904, left, and in 1907, right. Percy used some of his postcards, which depicted local events and people, to send to friends, especially to Willie Crowther, who lived at Luneburg, Germany. The following messages written to Willie tell us something about Percy:

21 May 1908. 'We have had a real good opera production by local artists in our town hall a few weeks ago. I have taken most of their photos.'

5 June 1908. 'Last Saturday, West Ardsley had their carnival. I snapped six groups and sold 300 postcards this week of them. Next Tuesday, one of my old flames gets wed and I am going to tea.'

2 August 1909. 'By gow, it has rained every day since Whitsuntide. Morley Feast is a fortnight today. Everybody is talking about going off for four days, so I think I might as well follow suit. I have planned to leave Hull on Feast Tuesday, 6p.m., arriving at Zeebrugge 7a.m. Wednesday morning. Returning from Zeebrugge Friday 8p.m., arriving at Hull 9a.m. Saturday. This will give me three clear days in which to see Belgium.'

5 November 1909, 'Trade is poor now. All the people are spending their money at the rink. Everyone is mad on it, except Percy. But I shall pull through.'

Percy also collected magazines to send to Willie. These included *Wide World*, *Strand* and *Story-Teller*, plus blood-and-thunders, detective tales and love tales.

Morley Amateur Operatic Society. Miriam White (standing) and Sarah Stevenson (kneeling) in *Sam Sings Opera*, at the town hall, April 1908. (A photograph by Percy Sykes.)

Miss Teale in the same production. The town hall also accommodated dramatic performances, orchestral concerts and piano recitals, to name but a few.

Dear W. & E.

This shows a bit of Adwalton Moor yesterday Mar 27/12. It will be like a rabbit burrow in a few days. They are all digging for coal, of course it is poor stuff to burn, but the best coal is now £4 a ton. Its a rum go and no mistake. P.S.

Coal picking, on Adwalton Moor. On 1 March 1912, an estimated one million miners went on strike nationwide to procure a guaranteed minimum wage. This led to coal picking from outcrops and spoil heaps. Here, shallow pits are being dug to reach poor quality fuel. Percy Sykes recorded the scene and made relevant comments.

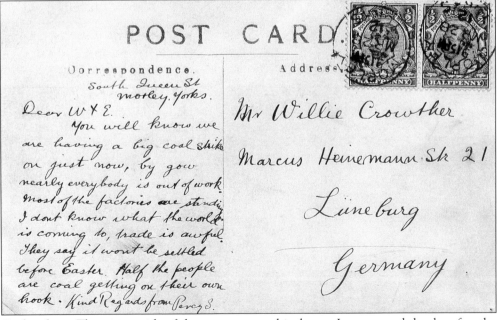

Coal picking. The reverse side of the upper postcard is shown. It was posted the day after the picture was taken, with more of Percy's pertinent comments. The strike ended in mid-April.

BEN TURNER

MORLEY

If yo miln pieces reit,
An' yo cuttle 'em streit,
    An' finish 'em fit for to wear.
Then yor wage sud be good,
An' yor wark sewerly sud
    Not leave yo o'er burdened wi care.

If yo spin yarn at's true,
Whether brahn, black, or blue,
    To mak into fine cloth bi'th mass.
Yo owt to be happy,
An' nivvur made snappy,
    Becos yon been crippled for brass.

If you weyve cloth correct,
Yon a reit ta expect,
    A dacent reward; it's what's due.
It's easy to win it,
Soa let us begin it,
    And each to each other be true.

B. T

Ben Turner (1863-1942). Born in Holmfirth, Turner eventually moved to Batley, from where he was actively engaged in trade unionism. For many years he served as secretary of the Heavy Woollen District Branch of the General Union of Textile Workers. When there was a strike at Hudson, Sykes & Bousfield's mill in about 1890, Turner wrote, 'We got a few more members and it looked as if Morley had been rushed into activity at last. Success was assured in the wages movement, but alas they soon slipped from membership when they had settled up their grievance.' Women were particularly reluctant to commit themselves to long-term membership, perhaps because of intimidation. At another (unnamed) Morley mill, Ben Turner and his supporters were expounding their views outside the mill yard as the weavers came out at tea time. Suddenly, sods were thrown from inside. Turner entered the yard to object, only to be forcibly ejected. It transpired that the sods had been thrown by the firm's foremen at the instigation of their employers. Twenty years later, relationships between mill employers and unions were less confrontational. On 19 July 1910, terms were agreed between a delegation from Morley cloth manufacturers and representatives of the General Union of Textile Workers, regarding hours and rates for willeyers and fettlers employed in Morley, Drighlington and Gildersome. The working week was to be 58 hours ($10 \frac{1}{2}$ hours on ordinary days and $5 \frac{1}{2}$ hours on Saturdays). Working times on Monday to Friday were to be 6a.m. to 6p.m. with $1 \frac{1}{2}$ hours for meals (presumably $\frac{1}{2}$ hour for breakfast and 1 hour for dinner). On Saturdays, 6a.m. to 12 noon (with $\frac{1}{2}$ hour for breakfast) were the hours to be worked. Rates of pay were $5 \frac{1}{2}$ d per hour, with $6 \frac{1}{4}$ d for overtime. The agreement was to stay in force until 1 October 1912. It was signed by representatives from both sides, including John Hartley for the employers and Ben Turner for the employees. Turner's pastime was composing dialect poems - the above example was penned with Morley textile workers in mind.

Morley committee members, Heavy Woollen District Branch of General Union of Textile Workers, 1917. Back row, from left to right: F. Smith, G.H. Wilson, G. Stead, G.G. Atack. Front row, from left to right: W. Firth, W. Walsh, J.W. Armitage, E. Auty, C. Auty. Wilson was also a member of Drighlington District Council, Armitage was on the committee of Morley Co-operative Society.

Tram accident, in Churwell, 12 May 1923. The picture looks towards Morley. After the driver experienced trouble with his brakes at the top of Churwell Hill, tramcar No. 191 careered down the one-in-eleven gradient, left the rails and overturned, causing the decks to separate. Six passengers were instantly killed and many more were injured. The car had to be scrapped.

Decorations, to celebrate Gildersome Carnival, *c.* 1907.

Welcome home! The large crowd is shown leaving St Paul's parish church, Drighlington, after the welcoming service for local servicemen on 28 June 1919. The church was built in 1878 on the site of an earlier one.